THE 21 TENETS OF
BIBLICAL
MASCULINITY

by Jerry Ross

Transitioning Young Men
From Boyhood to Manhood

Ultimate Goal Publications
Jasonville, Indiana
www.stayinthecastle.com

All Scripture from the King James Bible.

INTRODUCTION

Biblical masculinity has all but disappeared in the modern day culture. Satan has systematically targeted the tenets of Biblical manhood, eliminating them one by one from our society. As a whole, we no longer are rearing young men. Thank God there are exceptions, but they are simply that – exceptions. The church of Jesus Christ must scripturally define, and purposefully re-instill the character qualities of Biblical masculinity back into our boys and young men.

The following Bible principles are the result of a study of what the Word of God has to say concerning "young men/man". From this study we observe twenty-one tenets of Biblical masculinity.

I am defining a "young man" as a male between the ages of 12 and 30 years of age.

Jerry Ross,
April, 2012

TABLE OF CONTENTS

Tenet 1: Young men must embrace opportunities to develop their natural strength in the performance of physical labor. — Page 11

Tenet 2: Young men should master a marketable, wage-earning trade in their youth. — Page 15

Tenet 3: Young men should be assigned jobs that require courage. — Page 17

Tenet 4: Young men should never abuse an assigned position of authority by using it for selfish gain or self-gratification. — Page 19

Tenet 5: Young men should be trained in proper communication. — Page 21

Tenet 6: Young men should not hesitate to draw their swords against evil. — Page 23

Tenet 7: A young man should seek counsel from his elders, not his peers. — Page 25

Tenet 8: Young men should consistently praise the Lord. — Page 27

Tenet 9: Young men should remember that, no matter how physically strong they are, a far superior, supernatural strength can be accessed by learning to wait upon the Lord. — Page 29

Tenet 10: Young men should seek God in their youth with the understanding that the God/young man relationship may be the most potent available to them in their lifetime. — Page 31

Tenet 11: A young man should seek his Spirit vision. — Page 33

Tenet 12: Young men should understand that God calls   Page 35
out, from their ranks, His prophets in every generation.

Tenet 13: Young men should learn from aged men the four   Page 37
disciplines of Christian maturity. (Disciplined Thinking,
Reputable Living, Pure Convictions, Excellent Speech)

Tenet 14: Young men should master three vital masculine   Page 45
skills. (Overcoming Satanic Attacks, Developing Spiritual
Strength, Internalizing Scriptural Truth)

Tenet 15: Young men must learn to face and defeat giants.   Page 53

Tenet 16: Young men must learn that there are sins linked   Page 55
to youthfulness that will cause them great struggles.

Tenet 17: A young man should practice chivalry.   Page 63

Tenet 18: A young man should marry in his youth, and   Page 67
should discover all of the pleasures of women through one
woman – the wife of his youth.

Tenet 19: Young men should understand the importance   Page 69
of bearing a yoke in their youth, and the danger of an unequal
yoke.

Tenet 20: Young men should counter the natural inclination   Page 71
of older men to undervalue their youthfulness by showing
stellar character in six important areas. (Excellent Speech,
Mature Behavior, Selfless Love, Good Attitude, Sincere Faith,
Wholesome Purity)

Tenet 21: Young men should absorb the wisdom   Page 73
found in the book of Proverbs

Conclusion   Page 75

Dedicated to my dad,
Robert Leo Ross
- in every Biblical sense, a man.

21 TENETS OF

BIBLICAL MASCULINITY

by Jerry Ross

Joel 2:7
They shall run like mighty men;
they shall climb the wall like men of war;
and they shall march every one on his ways,
and they shall not break their ranks:

1 Corinthians 16:13
Watch ye, stand fast in the faith,
quit you like men, be strong.

Young man: defined as a male between
12 and 30 years of age .

TENET 1

Young men must embrace opportunities to develop their natural strength in the performance of physical labor.

*Proverbs 20:29 The glory of **young men** is their strength: and the beauty of old men is the grey head.*

When our wonderful Creator formed the first man's body, He wired within it the DNA that would provide for every generation a crop of strong, young men. Young man, your strength is your glory. It is one of the primary traits that differs you from the fairer yet weaker female gender. The primary purpose of your increasing strength is not so you can stand in front of the mirror and flex — but so that you can use it for the joy of physical labor.

Bible Examples for Young Men

*Genesis 18:7 And Abraham ran unto the herd, and fetched a calf tender and good, and gave it unto **a young man**; and he hasted to dress it.*

Abraham picked the calf, but a young man labored to prepare it. A feeder calf weighs between three and four hundred pounds. This was no small job.

*Genesis 22:3-5 And Abraham rose up early in the morning, and saddled his ass, and took two of his **young men** with him, and Isaac his son, and clave the wood for the burnt offering, and rose up, and went unto the place of which God had told him. Then on the third day Abraham lifted up his eyes, and saw the place afar off. And Abraham said unto his **young men**, Abide ye here with the ass; and I and the lad will go yonder and worship, and come again to you.*

11

Abraham took two "young men" with him. Abraham rode his donkey and the young men carried the wood for the burnt offering. Their youthful strength was put to use. It would have been unthinkable for them to expect an older man to perform this hard task. They honored Abraham by stepping up and doing the difficult. Later they were assigned the task of guarding Abraham's donkey – a mundane but important job that developed their patience as well as their protective skills.

*Exodus 24:4-5 And Moses wrote all the words of the LORD, and rose up early in the morning, and builded an altar under the hill, and twelve pillars, according to the twelve tribes of Israel. And he sent **young men** of the children of Israel, which offered burnt offerings, and sacrificed peace offerings of oxen unto the LORD.*

Young men were used to performing the physically taxing jobs involved in the slaughter and offering of oxen unto the LORD. Most young men in this culture have never been involved in butchering and processing cattle, but I can assure you, it is hard work. The oxen mentioned in this story weighed over a ton (2000 lbs).

*1 Samuel 26:22 And David answered and said, Behold the king's spear! and let one of the **young men** come over and fetch it.*

It was a young man who was sent to run and fetch, not an elder. David did not (nor would anyone in this time period of manliness) expect an older man to run and fetch while a young man stood and watched.

*Acts 5:5-10 And Ananias hearing these words fell down, and gave up the ghost: and great fear came on all them that heard these things. And the **young men** arose, wound him up, and carried him out, and buried him. And it was about the space of three hours after, when his wife, not knowing what was done, came in. And Peter answered unto her, Tell me whether ye sold the land for so much? And she said, Yea, for so much. Then Peter said unto her, How is it that ye have agreed* *together to tempt the Spirit of the Lord? behold, the feet of them which have buried thy husband are at the door, and shall carry thee out. Then fell she down straightway at his feet, and yielded up the ghost: and the* **young men** *came in, and found her dead, and, carrying her forth, buried her by her husband.*

It was young men, in the early church, who bound up and carried the "dead weight" of two corpses, dug the graves, and buried the dead. Again, this was hard work that required the glory of youthful strength. Young man, for you to ever lay claim to masculinity, you must be willing to embrace opportunities to perform hard, physical labor.

Shirking or Working?

If you shirk work, you are not a young man, you are a boy.

A boy views hard work as something to be avoided. He will sneak away and hide while others jump in and help. The change from boyhood to manhood is a change in the way you view labor. A *boy* feels like he has "won" if he gets out of work. A *man* feels cheated if he was denied the opportunity to help.

I have watched senior saints — elderly men and women — carry chairs and tables, mop floors and take out bags of trash after a church fellowship while teen boys loitered outside. I said teen *boys*. A young *man* would never allow this to happen. He would not only help, he would try to convince the elder saints to let him do it for them. If they refused, he would quicken his pace, and increase his load to see to it that he did the vast majority of the work. He would glory in his strength.

Some boys pretend manliness when in public, but are shamefully slothful in their own homes. Should your dad work hard for eight or ten hours, then come home and mow the lawn while you play video games in your room? Should your mom, in addition to her daily tasks, still have to find the time to clean your room or pick up your dirty laundry? Son, it is time to transition from boyhood to manhood!

The Apostle Paul must have heard reports of laziness within the congregation of the church in Thessalonica. Notice his admonition in his first letter, followed by a stern rebuke in his second letter.

1 Thessalonians 4:11 And that ye study to be quiet, and to do your own business, and to work with your own hands, as we commanded you;

2 Thessalonians 3:6-12 Now we command you, brethren, in the name of our Lord Jesus Christ, that ye withdraw yourselves from every brother that walketh disorderly, and not after the tradition which he received of us.....For even when we were with you, this we commanded you, that if any would not work, neither should he eat. For we hear that there are some which walk among you disorderly, working not at all, but are busybodies. Now them that are such we command and exhort by our Lord Jesus Christ, that with quietness they work, and eat their own bread.

By divine inspiration, Paul pens the words of God — God's viewpoint on this matter of laziness. In God's view, if you do not work, you should not eat. Period. Not only that, God sees you as disorderly (def: insubordinate, unruly) and declares you a busybody. God also commands good brethren to withdraw from your company. This shunning is done in hopes of shaming you into correcting your laziness.

If you shirk work, you will soon gain a shameful reputation among real men. Work is the proving ground of manhood. It provides its own reward. A man who enthusiastically embraces a job can rejoice both in the work, and after the work — for he will experience the joy of true, biblical masculinity.

Galatians 6:4-5 But let every man prove his own work, and then shall he have rejoicing in himself alone, and not in another. For every man shall bear his own burden.

TENET 2

Young men should master a marketable, wage-earning trade in their youth.

*Genesis 46:34 That ye shall say, Thy servants' trade hath been about cattle **from our youth** even until now, both we, and also our fathers:*

Mark 6:3 Is not this the carpenter, the son of Mary,

Matthew 13:55 Is not this the carpenter's son?

In my book, *The Teenage Years of Jesus Christ*, I provide an in-depth, biblical study of the six attributes of Christ during his "young man" years. They are as follows:

1. The Teenage Christ increased in wisdom.
2. The Teenage Christ increased in maturity.
3. The Teenage Christ increased in favor with men.
4. The Teenage Christ increased in favor with God.
5. The Teenage Christ remained submissive to Joseph and Mary.
6. The Teenage Christ mastered a skilled trade.

In the before mentioned book, an entire chapter is devoted to Christ's example of mastering a marketable, skilled trade in his youth. In that chapter I write:

"Before Jesus was a preacher, he was a carpenter. Before he ever healed the sick or raised the dead, He carefully crafted carts and cabinets. His hands were calloused. His biceps were knotted with the strength of hard labor. He rose up early each morning and worked beside Joseph, learning the skills of a craftsman. These skills were mastered during his teenage years."

In the first tenet, I encouraged you to develop a work ethic. But if a young man learns to work, yet fails to develop a marketable skill, it will be difficult for him to earn a living. Your youthful strength must be harnessed and trained to perform a skilled trade.

The Jewish culture understood the need for a young man to learn a skilled trade. When a young man reached the age of twelve, he became an apprentice to his father or another trusted male relative. Under said tutelage, he mastered a wage-earning skill. To this day, there is this saying in Jewish culture — *"He who fails to teach his son a trade, rears a thief"*. It is thievery to be able-bodied yet live off the government. The government generates no money. It taxes those who work hard, taking from them the fruit of their labor. For that hard-earned money to be handed to a man who refuses to work, or who was foolish enough not to learn a trade, is criminal.

Mastering money-saving, wage-earning skills starts with working beside your father around the home. This will teach you home maintenance, vehicle maintenance, and common sense. If your dad is working on something, jump in and help! Also, you should learn the basics of your father's trade, both by discussing it with him, and working with him when possible.

Look around your church and find men who have wage-earning skills. Seek out opportunities for summer employment. If they cannot afford to hire you, it would still be to your advantage to volunteer to help them. Your pay is the knowledge and skills you are gaining.

Set as your goal to master one wage-earning skill during your young man years. Even if this trade is not what you end up doing for the rest of your life, it will always give you something to fall back on.

A wage-earning skill will place you in a position to be able to one day provide for a family of your own. No young man has a right to ask a father for his daughter's hand in marriage, without first being in a position to financially provide for her. And no young man can claim biblical masculinity who does not provide his own way in this world.

TENET 3

Young men should be assigned jobs that require courage.

*Joshua 6:22-23 But Joshua had said unto the two men that had spied out the country, Go into the harlot's house, and bring out thence the woman, and all that she hath, as ye sware unto her. And the **young men** that were spies went in, and brought out Rahab, and her father, and her mother, and her brethren, and all that she had; and they brought out all her kindred, and left them without the camp of Israel.*

The two spies that were sent to spy out Canaan-land were young men. They were selected for a task that required courage, cunning, and personal risk. They had to make decisions based on their ability to read people – who to trust and who to avoid. They entered a walled and guarded city, evaluated the strengths and weaknesses, spent a day hiding in the roof material of a harlot's home, and returned safely to report to Joshua.

*1 Samuel 17:33-35 And Saul said to David, Thou art not able to go against this Philistine to fight with him: for **thou art but a youth**, and he a man of war from his youth. And David said unto Saul, Thy servant kept his father's sheep, and there came a lion, and a bear, and took a lamb out of the flock: And I went out after him, and smote him, and delivered it out of his mouth: and when he arose against me, I caught him by his beard, and smote him, and slew him.*

A young man volunteered for a job that required great courage. This was not the first time David needed courage. He was first proven a man while in solitude, choosing to face a lion, then a bear in protection of his father's sheep.

Courage is not the absence of fear, but a calm conquering of your fear as you focus on doing what needs to be done. This fear is con-

17

quered by trusting the Lord. This lion/bear/giant killer later penned these words:

Psalms 56:3 What time I am afraid, I will trust in thee.

In the face of danger, biblical masculinity performs its duty with a whispered prayer followed by manly resolve. Early in life, you have to learn to face your fears.

Courage is an essential ingredient of authentic manhood. There is no place for cowardice in God's service. Young man, do not confuse courage with cockiness. Courage does not go out looking for confrontation, neither does it seek out foolish danger. Had the lion and bear left his sheep alone, David would have left them alone.

Courage is also an essential ingredient in proper leadership. Many times a right decision is not a popular decision. A leader must please God above anyone else. God exhorted Joshua, the new leader of Israel thus:

Joshua 1:6 Be strong and of a good courage...

Joshua 1:7 Only be thou strong and very courageous, that thou mayest observe to do according to all the law, which Moses my servant commanded thee: turn not from it to the right hand or to the left, that thou mayest prosper whithersoever thou goest.

Joshua 1:9 Have not I commanded thee? Be strong and of a good courage; be not afraid, neither be thou dismayed: for the LORD thy God is with thee whithersoever thou goest.

Joshua could be courageous because God was on his side. Joshua was fulfilling God's calling, obeying God's Word, and because of that, could count on God's protection and promises.

A boy quakes in the face of danger. But a young man quiets his fears, focuses his resolve, trusts the Lord, and then does his duty.

TENET 4

Young men should never abuse an assigned position of authority by using it for selfish gain or self-gratification.

*1 Samuel 2:12-17, 22 Now the sons of Eli were sons of Belial; they knew not the LORD. And the priests' custom with the people was, that, when any man offered sacrifice, the priest's servant came, while the flesh was in seething, with a fleshhook of three teeth in his hand; And he struck it into the pan, or kettle, or caldron, or pot; all that the fleshhook brought up the priest took for himself. So they did in Shiloh, unto all the Israelites that came thither. Also before they burnt the fat, the priest's servant came, and said to the man that sacrificed, Give flesh to roast for the priest; for he will not have sodden flesh of thee, but raw. And if any man said unto him, Let them not fail to burn the fat presently, and then take as much as thy soul desireth; then he would answer him, Nay; but thou shalt give it me now: and if not, I will take it by force. Wherefore **the sin of the young men** was very great before the LORD: for men abhorred the offering of the LORD......Now Eli was very old, and heard all that his sons did unto all Israel; and how they lay with the women that assembled at the door of the tabernacle of the congregation.*

Eli the priest made a grave error in the rearing of his sons. He allowed them — at an early age — a position of authority without proper oversight and accountability. When he "heard all that his sons did" the Bible goes on to say in I Samuel 3:13, "he restrained them not".

Hophni and Phinehas (Eli's sons) were still young men. They did not have the maturity to understand true leadership. They saw a trusted position as an opportunity for selfish gain and self-gratification. They mistook leadership as an opportunity to force or manipulate people into serving and satisfying them, instead of seeing leadership as a sacred opportunity to serve the Lord and others.

As a young man, you will be given opportunities to lead. Leadership is a sacred trust. It is a great sin to abuse authoritative opportunities.

Your assigned opportunity to lead should be carefully monitored by older, wiser men. There have been far too many scandals in our fundamental churches that were the result of a pastor who placed a young man too early (or without proper accountability) into a position of authority. Too many times, when that young man proved himself unworthy of the position, he was allowed to remain or was "reassigned" to a different leadership position where his character flaws again were displayed. Sadly, like Eli, too many times the pastor turned a blind eye because the young man was his son or relative.

Any young man entrusted with a position of authority who abuses that position for selfish gain or self-gratification should immediately be stripped of that position. He should also be properly punished for whatever infractions occurred. He has proven himself a boy, instead of a man — and boys shouldn't lead.

Leadership is to be carried out in a selfless sincere manner. A godly leader does not make decisions based on what is best for him, but instead what is best for the followers.

TENET 5

Young men should be trained in proper communication.

*1 Samuel 25:5-9 And David sent out **ten young men**, and David said unto **the young men**, Get you up to Carmel, and go to Nabal, and greet him in my name: And thus shall ye say to him that liveth in prosperity, Peace be both to thee, and peace be to thine house, and peace be unto all that thou hast. And now I have heard that thou hast shearers: now thy shepherds which were with us, we hurt them not, neither was there ought missing unto them, all the while they were in Carmel. Ask thy **young men**, and they will show thee. Wherefore let the **young men** find favour in thine eyes: for we come in a good day: give, I pray thee, whatsoever cometh to thine hand unto thy servants, and to thy son David. And when David's **young men** came, they spake to Nabal according to all those words in the name of David, and ceased.*

King David needed to get a message to Nabal. He assigned the responsibility of the communication to ten young men. David could have gone himself, but I believe that King David took this opportunity to teach ten young men how to respectfully converse and accurately convey an important message.

Notice the break down of the communication.

"....greet him in my name." They were to be clear that the communication be properly identified as coming from King David. They came as representatives of the king.

"And thus shall ye say to him...." David gives them a word for word message. As a young man, when you are trusted to communicate a message from one authority to another, you should be careful to listen to the exact wording of the communication. The ability to accurately convey an assigned message is essential.

"Peace be both to thee, and peace be to thine house, and peace be

unto all that thou hast." Notice the time taken to properly and respectfully address an elder. Any communication should be preceded by kind words and well wishes. David was teaching his young men an important lesson: as a young man, you should always take the time to show respect and kindness to another man.

"And now I have heard that thou hast shearers......Wherefore let the young men find favour in thine eyes: for we come in a good day: give, I pray thee, whatsoever cometh to thine hand unto thy servants, and to thy son David." The rest of the communication is then given. Notice the tone of respect. It is a humble request, not a demand. David sent through these ten young men a well-worded, respectful request that assumed nothing; but instead placed himself and his young men as servants to Nabal, allowing Nabal to decide the extent of generosity offered.

There is a difference between entreating and rebuking.

1 Timothy 5:1 Rebuke not an elder, but entreat him as a father...

Too many boys, who fancy themselves young men, fail in this area of masculine communication skills. If you are a smart mouth, you are a boy, not a man. If you sass your parents or other authority figures, you are placing on display your immaturity. King David taught his young men how to respectfully communicate to grown men.

"And when David's young men came, they spake to Nabal according to all those words in the name of David, and ceased." Notice the young men relayed the words of David, in his name, then ceased. Never embellish a trusted communication. Relay the message then stop talking. Many times a communication is misunderstood because the person relaying the message adds facts or assumptions that were never intended to be a part of the message.

Young men who are properly trained in communication skills make great candidates for the Gospel ministry! Review this chapter. How might these principles relate to the delivery of a Bible sermon?

TENET 6

A young man should not hesitate to draw his sword against evil.

1 Samuel 1:14-15 And David said unto him, How wast thou not afraid to stretch forth thine hand to destroy the LORD'S anointed? And David called **one of the young men***, and said, Go near, and fall upon him. And he smote him that he died.*

The latter part of King Saul's reign was marked by jealousy and insecurity against David. King Saul hated him, haunted him, and hunted him. Twice, while Saul sought for David, God allowed David opportunity to kill Saul. Twice, David could have taken Saul's life. But David understood a principle — you do not lift up your hand against divinely appointed authority.

When the news came of Saul and Jonathan's death, from David's lips is delivered a tender and gracious epitaph (II Samuel 1:17-27). He also delivered swift justice to the Amalekite who claimed to have slain Saul. David called to one of his young men to "fall upon" this messenger with a sword. The Amalekite died that day because he had dared to lift up his sword against God's anointed leader of Israel.

Young man, there are times to draw your sword against evil.

God's appointed leader for every home is the father. A young man who stands passively by while someone mocks, disobeys or ridicules his father is not a man, but a boy. God's anointed leader for your church is your pastor. A *boy* stands mute mouth while others seek to slay his pastor with their tongues, but a *man* draws his sword! Never lift up your hand against God's appointed authority (whether it be a Sunday School teacher, your youth pastor, your boss, etc.), and never let any other man stand in your presence and do it unchallenged.

2 Samuel 18:15 And **ten young men** *that bare Joab's armour compassed about and smote Absalom, and slew him.*

Absalom's name is synonymous with rebellion. In a premeditated fashion, he stood outside a gate of Jerusalem and subtly criticized and steadily undermined his father's authority. He turned the hearts of men away from God's appointed leader and towards himself.

Joab, David's captain of the host, sought out this rebel in battle and found him hanging in a tree by the symbol of his rebellious heart — his long flowing hair. Joab thrust three darts into the heart of Absalom, and then encouraged his young men to finish the job. Young men drew their swords and slew a rebel.

Boys tolerate and/or sadly idolize rebels. *Men* confront them with drawn swords. The Bible says that rebellion is *"as the sin of witchcraft"* (I Samuel 15:23). Rebellion is satanic and should never be tolerated by a real man.

*Judges 8:20-21 And he said unto Jether his firstborn, Up, and slay them. But **the youth drew not his sword: for he feared, because he was yet a youth**. Then Zebah and Zalmunna said, Rise thou, and fall upon us: for as the man is, so is his strength. And Gideon arose, and slew Zebah and Zalmunna, and took away the ornaments that were on their camels' necks.*

Two heathen kings, Zebah and Zalmunna, reigned over Midian. The Midianites were the avowed enemies of Israel. They had oppressed and defiled the people of God. After God delivered them into the hand of Gideon and his three hundred warriors, Gideon instructed his son, Jether, to draw his sword and slay these wicked kings. Jether lacked the courage to do so. He was even taunted by these enemies of God who encouraged him to play the man, but because of his youthfulness, fear stayed his hand. Gideon steps up and slays them while his son, Jether, watches in fear — and we never again hear mentioned, in the Scriptures, the name of Jether.

Satan is the enemy of Christ. He is the original rebel and has vowed to destroy the church of the living God. *Boys* cower in fear, and refuse to fight his influences. Some even turn traitor, choosing to live their lives joining Satan in hurting the work of God.

Real men fight the enemy of Christ. Real men draw their swords.

TENET 7

A young man should seek counsel from his elders, not his peers.

*1 Kings 12:8 But he (Rehoboam) forsook the counsel of the old men, which they had given him, and consulted with **the young men** that were grown up with him, and which stood before him:*

Rehoboam was the son of King Solomon. Upon the death of his father, Rehoboam inherited his father's throne, but sadly, not his father's wisdom. He had access to much of that wisdom through both his father's writings and his father's peers. The "old men" who had served with Solomon tried to give him sound and sage advice. This young king forsook their counsel and turned his ears to his peers. These *young men* possessed no greater wisdom than Rehoboam — they were his contemporaries and thus they simply mirrored his knowledge and experience. Yet he chose to follow their untested advice. As a result, a nation was plunged into civil war.

*2 Kings 6:17 And Elisha prayed, and said, LORD, I pray thee, open his eyes, that he may see. And the LORD opened the eyes of **the young man**; and he saw: and, behold, the mountain was full of horses and chariots of fire round about Elisha.*

This young man, who was a servant to Elisha, learned that the older, godly man could see things that he was not yet able to see. One of the reasons that a young man should seek counsel from older, more experienced men is that they have a perspective he has not been afforded. Their spiritual, experienced eyes can see what youthfulness cannot.

One of the downfalls of young men in our society is that they have developed a foolish dedication and arrogant loyalty to their peers. A friend's opinion usually trumps a parent's opinion. What their girl-

25

friends think is more important than what their pastor thinks. Because of this, unwise decisions have become the norm. No matter how flippant your attitude may have become, you would be wise to remember that poor decisions result in real life, long-ranging consequences. Yes, you may choose what you do, but you do not get to choose the consequences of what you do — they are built in.

Young man, your father knows more than you in most every area of importance. Your grandfather has forgotten more than you presently know! Your pastor has special spiritual insight and wisdom. Older, godly men in your church can provide you with a great multitude of counselors. Wise is the young man who engages regularly with older men.

Proverbs 20:5 Counsel in the heart of man is like deep water; but a man of understanding will draw it out.

Let me give you a general observation: beware of the one who is quick to give advice. It probably isn't worth much. Wise counsel is like deep water. It exists in the hearts of godly and aged men and if you want to access it, you will have to draw it out.

Learn to treasure the wisdom won by spiritual and practiced experience. Never make a major decision in your life without seeking godly counsel.

Proverbs 15:22 Without counsel purposes are disappointed: but in the multitude of counsellors they are established.

Proverbs 24:6 For by wise counsel thou shalt make thy war: and in multitude of counsellors there is safety.

Proverbs 12:15 The way of a fool is right in his own eyes: but he that hearkeneth unto counsel is wise.

TENET 8

Young men should consistently praise the Lord.

*Psalms 148:1, 12-13 Praise ye the LORD. Praise ye the LORD from the heavens: praise him in the heights.....Both **young men**, and maidens; old men, and children: Let them praise the name of the LORD: for his name alone is excellent; his glory is above the earth and heaven.*

Young man, when was the last time you praised the Lord? God is worthy of our praise. It is masculine to praise the Lord. The Bible specifically lists it as one of the responsibilities of young men. A real man understands that God should be constantly and verbally credited for all of the good which He bestows upon each of us.

Many times a day, you should say the words, "Praise the Lord."

Psalms 119:164 Seven times a day do I praise thee because of thy righteous judgments.

Silence in this area is near blasphemy. When you are blessed, or something falls your way, acknowledge God as the source of that goodness. Never be ashamed to publicly praise the Lord. Do it in front of others. The more you praise the Lord, the more reasons He will give you to praise Him!

Psalms 7:17 I will praise the LORD according to his righteousness: and will sing praise to the name of the LORD most high.

Psalms 21:13 Be thou exalted, LORD, in thine own strength: so will we sing and praise thy power.

Psalms 28:7 The LORD is my strength and my shield; my heart trusted in him, and I am helped: therefore my heart greatly rejoiceth; and with my song will I praise him.

Psalms 40:3 And he hath put a new song in my mouth, even praise unto our God: many shall see it, and fear, and shall trust in the LORD.

These verses are a mere sampling of those found in Psalms exhorting us to praise the Lord through song. Young men should never shy from singing boldly for the Lord. Only someone ignorant of the scriptures would suggest that singing is not masculine. Some of the most wonderful and powerful times of worship I have experienced in my life have been with a room full of men, as we together sang boldly our praise to our God!

Sing out during the congregational song service. Join your church choir if you can. Both publicly and privately, sing praises to your God.

Psalms 44:8 In God we boast all the day long, and praise thy name for ever. Selah.

I believe Psalms 44:8 places its finger on the reason most young men struggle with praising God. The reason is *pride*! The same young man who will not praise the Lord is usually the same young man who boasts in himself. When you are blessed or when you are allowed to accomplish something, you will either boast in yourself or boast in the Lord. A secure young man realizes that nothing is accomplished outside of the mercy, grace and strength of God. Youthful pride wants praise for self. Manly maturity is secure enough and humble enough to give God the glory He is due.

Psalms 107:8 Oh that men would praise the LORD for his goodness, and for his wonderful works to the children of men!

TENET 9

Young men should remember that no matter how physically strong they are, a far superior supernatural strength can be accessed by learning to wait upon the Lord.

*Proverbs 20:29 The glory of **young men** is their strength: and the beauty of old men is the grey head.*

*Isaiah 40:30-31 Even **the youths** shall faint and be weary, and the **young men** shall utterly fall: But they that wait upon the LORD shall renew their strength; they shall mount up with wings as eagles; they shall run, and not be weary; and they shall walk, and not faint.*

Most young men are naturally strong. They are also impatient. The idea of "waiting" holds no attraction to the young. Youth wants to be active, to go, to do. It takes greater discipline for a young man to schedule time each day to wait upon the Lord.

The phrase "wait upon the Lord" is found four times in the Bible. To *wait upon* means *to twist together* or *to collect.* Spending time with God each morning, and choosing to walk with God each day *twists together* His immortal strength with your mortal limitations. It allows you *to collect* His wisdom, His guidance and His direction so that your human labors and efforts accomplish much more than you could ever accomplish laboring in your own wisdom and strength.

The young man wise enough, and humble enough, to acknowledge his need for God's power will run laps around the carnal or worldly youth who operates exclusively in his own power. He will understand that time spent in God's Word each morning will benefit him in everything he must accomplish that day. Prayer time, for the wise young man, is power time! Waiting upon God will provide that young man with supernatural wisdom, strength, and endurance. It will also protect him from unwise decisions that sap hours from his day, and add frustration to his mind.

Time spent waiting before the Lord each day should include time spent doing the following:

1. **Praising God.** Just spend some time telling God how great He is and acknowledging before Him how much you need Him.
2. **Praying before God.** Ask God for the things you will need to be effective that day. Pray for wisdom, spiritual strength, boldness for God, and protection from temptation.
3. **Seeking wisdom from the Scriptures.** Every young man should read some from the book of Proverbs each day. Read prayerfully, asking God to impart to you of His wisdom.
4. **Emptying oneself of sin and self.** A time of confession and a deliberate dying to self before God will ready you for being filled with the Holy Spirit.
5. **Seeking the filling of the Holy Spirit.** Ask for it. Claim it by faith. Seek direction from the Holy Spirit through out the day.

Immaturity runs ahead in its own strength, with disdain towards those "spiritual types" who wait before the Lord. But immaturity is always outrun, outwitted and outworked by the young man who chooses to operate in the power and wisdom of the Spirit of God.

Psalms 37:9 For evildoers shall be cut off: but those that wait upon the LORD, they shall inherit the earth.

Psalms 123 Unto thee lift I up mine eyes, O thou that dwellest in the heavens. Behold, as the eyes of servants look unto the hand of their masters, and as the eyes of a maiden unto the hand of her mistress; so our eyes wait upon the LORD our God, until that he have mercy upon us. Have mercy upon us, O LORD, have mercy upon us: for we are exceedingly filled with contempt. Our soul is exceedingly filled with the scorning of those that are at ease, and with the contempt of the proud.

TENET 10

Young men should seek God in their youth with the understanding that the God/young man relationship may be the most potent available to them in their life.

*Job 29:1-4 Moreover Job continued his parable, and said, Oh that I were as in months past, as in the days when God preserved me; When his candle shined upon my head, and when by his light I walked through darkness; As I was in **the days of my youth**, when the secret of God was upon my tabernacle;*

*Psalms 71:16-17 I will go in the strength of the Lord GOD: I will make mention of thy righteousness, even of thine only. O God, thou hast taught me **from my youth**: and hitherto have I declared thy wondrous works.*

*Ecclesiastes 12:1 Remember now thy Creator in **the days of thy youth**, while the evil days come not, nor the years draw nigh, when thou shalt say, I have no pleasure in them;*

In the above verses, we have divinely preserved for us the testimonies of three men. All three reminisce about the God/young man relationship that each enjoyed in their youth.

Job remembers the days of his youth, *"when the secret of God was upon my tabernacle."* He describes the relationship that he enjoyed with God in his youth thus, *"when his candle shined upon my head, and when by his light I walked through darkness."* Job remembered the intimacy of God's presence, the glowing effect it had upon his countenance, and the clarity of direction it brought each day.

David remembers the sweet times of intimate instruction that he received as a young man who sought out God in his youth. He points back to it as the foundation upon which he now stands in his aged

31

years and, from that platform, he now declares the wonderful works of God.

Solomon, as an old man, recounts his youthful days and the choice he made to focus them on God. We find these words in *Ecclesiastes*, the third and final book God allowed him to write. (Should we be shocked that his first book — written in his youth — was *The Song of Solomon*, written with almost embarrassing intimacy as he describes his heart's journey to God?) In his old age, he urges young men to remember their Creator in the days of their youth. He begs us not to miss those unique and sweet years with God. He goes on to warn us that there are evil days ahead when we will need the memory of pursuing God in our youth!

I am fifty years old as I write this book to you. Let me assure you that I would not trade the relationship I have with God now for the one I had in my youth. I will also quickly add two things. First, I do not believe I would have the depth of the relationship I now have with God had I not pursued God in my youth. Secondly, the relationship I have now is *not* the same as then — it cannot be — but in some ways THEN was the most amazing of the years of our walk together.

There is something about the youthful heart that can never be reproduced. There is something about a young man's relationship with God that is uniquely blessed. Maybe it is the fact that we feel everything so deeply in our youth. Maybe it is that there are so many "firsts" as our relationship with God grows. I don't know. Maybe our faith is simpler, life is simpler — maybe it is all of these things. I do know this — if you miss out on walking with God in your youth, you may very well be missing out on the sweetest and most potent moments you will ever have in His presence.

Job would tell you that you will be glad you gave God your youth when the testing days come. David would tell you that if you miss God in your youth, you are missing a foundation that you may never regain. I believe King Solomon would tell you, "Remember NOW thy creator, in the days of thy youth." I imagine he might go on to whisper, with a tear on his cheek, "I wish I could go back and experience those days one more time."

And I would concur.

TENET 11

A young man should seek his Spirit vision.

*Joel 2:28-29 And it shall come to pass afterward, that I will pour out my spirit upon all flesh; and **your sons** and your daughters shall prophesy, your old men shall dream dreams, **your young men** shall see visions: And also upon the servants and upon the handmaids in those days will I pour out my spirit.*

*Acts 2:14-18 But Peter, standing up with the eleven, lifted up his voice, and said unto them, Ye men of Judaea, and all ye that dwell at Jerusalem, be this known unto you, and hearken to my words: For these are not drunken, as ye suppose, seeing it is but the third hour of the day. But this is that which was spoken by the prophet Joel; And it shall come to pass in the last days, saith God, I will pour out of my Spirit upon all flesh: and **your sons** and your daughters shall prophesy, and **your young men** shall see visions, and your old men shall dream dreams: And on my servants and on my handmaidens I will pour out in those days of my Spirit; and they shall prophesy:*

In the verses above, we see both the prophesy of the outpouring of God's Spirit upon human flesh, and the fulfillment of said prophecy. Young man, let me point out the details of this promise:

1. God's spirit will be poured out on "all flesh"; both "servants" and "handmaids" will receive the indwelling of the Holy Spirit.
2. As a result, both "sons" and "daughters" will prophesy (witness).
3. Young men shall "see visions".
4. Old men shall "dream dreams".

Although young ladies are indwelt by the Spirit and can be potentially filled with the Spirit, and although young ladies can also be involved in Spirit-empowered soul winning, when it comes to visions and dreams, we enter exclusively into a man's world.

Since men have been called to leadership (yes, it is Biblical, so let me say it again), since MEN are called to spiritual and practical leadership, it is important that we receive from the Holy Spirit not only an indwelling and a filling, but a *vision* of what we are to accomplish.

Sometime during your "young man" years, the Holy Spirit of God will reveal to you your *Spirit vision*. Don't let that phrase confuse you. Yes, I am part Indian — my grandmother being a quarter part Choctaw — but I can assure you that I am not speaking of some pagan religious practice. Your "Spirit vision" occurs when the Holy Spirit reveals to you the purpose for your creation — literally, the direction of God's divine will for your life, programmed into you while He formed you in your mother's womb.

Jeremiah 1:4-5 Then the word of the LORD came unto me, saying, Before I formed thee in the belly I knew thee; and before thou camest forth out of the womb I sanctified thee, and I ordained thee a prophet unto the nations.

God came to Jeremiah in his youth, and revealed to him the reason God created him. We generally refer to this story as "Jeremiah's call to preach", but I believe that might be an underestimation of what happened. God did not just *call* Jeremiah to preach as a young man, He *created* Jeremiah to preach from his mother's womb. Then God later gave Jeremiah — in his "young man" years — his Spirit vision.

Young man, no one is here by accident. The same God Who formed Jeremiah, formed you in your mother's womb. He has already equipped you and sanctified you for specific purposes, great moments and divine appointments. To live and die without discovering and fulfilling that supernatural plan is to live a wasted life.

I am not saying that you are to be a preacher. I am saying that you are here to discover a divine plan. You can only discover that plan as you surrender *your will* for *God's will*. Once you surrender to God's will, you must wait upon the Lord, and sometime in the waiting, you will be given your Spirit vision.

I can tell you no more. The rest must come straight from Him.

TENET 12

Young men should understand that God calls out, from their ranks, His prophets in every generation

*Amos 2:10-12 Also I brought you up from the land of Egypt, and led you forty years through the wilderness, to possess the land of the Amorite. And I raised up **of your sons** for prophets, and **of your young men** for Nazarites. Is it not even thus, O ye children of Israel? saith the LORD. But ye gave the Nazarites wine to drink; and commanded the prophets, saying, Prophesy not.*

As you seek your Spirit vision, God may reveal to you that His purpose and plan is for you to be a preacher. This should not come as a shock. God has called preachers from the ranks of young men in every generation.

As I said in the last chapter, the call to preach is really just a revealing of what has always been. Young men are not just called to preach, they were created to preach from their mother's womb. It is foreordained, predetermined, and the calling is without repentance.

Rom. 11:29 For the gifts and calling of God are without repentance.

What "without repentance" means is that God will not change His mind about your call. You were ordained and sanctified from your mother's womb. You can run from it, but you cannot erase it. You can ruin it by disqualifying yourself, but by doing so you doom yourself to the unhappiest of all lives — a life lived being on the inside something you can never be on the outside.

If this is your calling and your purpose, then embrace it. You are blessed! It is not something to dread, it is the greatest of all honors. Think of it! You get to spend your life preaching the Word of God! Shortly after my call to peach (August 7, 1979), God secured for me my life verse:

Ephesians 3:8 Unto me, who am less than the least of all saints, is this grace given, that I should preach among the Gentiles the unsearchable riches of Christ;

The call to preach is not something that should produce pride, but instead a humble acceptance of a sacred grace given. It is also something for which you must prepare.

1 Timothy 3:1-7 This is a true saying, If a man desire the office of a bishop, he desireth a good work. A bishop then must be blameless, the husband of one wife, vigilant, sober, of good behaviour, given to hospitality, apt to teach; Not given to wine, no striker, not greedy of filthy lucre; but patient, not a brawler, not covetous; One that ruleth well his own house, having his children in subjection with all gravity; (For if a man know not how to rule his own house, how shall he take care of the church of God?) Not a novice, lest being lifted up with pride he fall into the condemnation of the devil. Moreover he must have a good report of them which are without; lest he fall into reproach and the snare of the devil.

As a young man, called into the Gospel ministry, your entire focus during these young man years is to develop the character traits that will qualify you to fulfill your calling. Study the above list along with what is added in Titus 1:5-9. Understand the Bible definition of each qualifying trait. These are not suggestions, they are qualifications! Until your character so aligns, you remain unqualified to fulfill your calling.

After Bible college, work under a senior pastor. Be an Elisha to some Elijah. Serve him, learn from him and get ready. There will be a day when the mantle will drop to you.

If you discover you are not called to preach, that does not make you a second-class Christian. If God has not called you to preach, ask Him to tie your heart to a man of God who is divinely called. Then use your unique gifts and talents to help him fulfill his vision.

TENET 13

Young men should learn from aged men the four disciplines of Christian maturity.

Titus 2:2-8 That the aged men be sober, grave, temperate, sound in faith, in charity, in patience.....Young men likewise exhort to be sober minded. In all things showing thyself a pattern of good works: in doctrine showing uncorruptness, gravity, sincerity, Sound speech, that cannot be condemned; that he that is of the contrary part may be ashamed, having no evil thing to say of you.

Titus chapter two begins by exhorting aged men and aged women to be godly and biblical in their conduct, then placing upon them the responsibility to teach the young men and the young women specific qualities. There are four disciplines of Christian maturity listed for the young man. Aged men are to teach you these things, but it is your responsibility to master these four disciplines early in your youth.

1. Disciplined thinking. *"...exhort to be sober minded..."*
2. Reputable living. *"In all things showing thyself a pattern of good works..."*
3. Pure convictions. *"...in doctrine showing uncorruptness, gravity, sincerity..."*
4. Excellent speech. *"Sound speech, that cannot be condemned..."*

These four disciplines define Christian maturity. If you are undisciplined in your mind, lax in your conduct, undeveloped or un-Biblical in your convictions, and do not know how to control your tongue, you are a boy, not a man.

Manhood is not defined by age, but by discipline. Sadly, we have a culture filled with teenage and twenty-something *boys*. If this is true of you, today you can begin to change that. At fifty years of age, I am well qualified as an "aged man", so let's look together at each of these disciplines and allow me to teach you how to master them.

Disciplined Thinking
"...exhort to be sober minded...."

Let me explain to you how God made you. You are a triune being: body, soul, and spirit. Your flesh is your main problem — it seldom wants to do right. If you are saved, your reborn spirit is your hope! Thank God that when you were saved, you became a new creature in Jesus Christ. So your flesh votes for carnality, your reborn spirit urges spirituality, and the tiebreaker is your soul.

Now, stay with me. Your soul is also a triune being. It consists of your mind (thoughts), your heart (emotions) and your will. Your mind is the key to everything! If your thinking is right, your emotions will be right, and your will chooses right. Get these three things right, and your soul is right! When your soul chooses right, it becomes the tie- breaker between your flesh and your reborn spirit. Reread this paragraph until you fully understand it.

Got it? If you disciplined your mind to stay with me, then you have already come to this conclusion: *the battleground for who you are is won or lost in your mind!*

That is why the Bible has instructed the aged men to teach the young man to be sober minded. "Sober" means to be self-controlled or disciplined in your thinking.

God has constructed our minds with this blessed characteristic: no man can think of more than one thing at a time! When a young man understands this, he learns how to eliminate wrong, immature or sinful thinking. To do this, he must be pro-active in choosing what he will think about throughout the day.

Replace daydreaming with diligent thoughts. You can let your mind drift, or take hold of your mental reins and direct it.

Psalms 119:113 I hate vain thoughts: but thy law do I love.
Jer 4:14 O Jerusalem, wash thine heart from wickedness, that thou mayest be saved. How long shall thy vain thoughts lodge within thee?

Proverbs 21:5 The thoughts of the diligent tend only to plenteousness;

David, a man after God's own heart, wrote how he hated vain thoughts. Vain means empty, undisciplined or unproductive. Jeremiah the prophet properly points out to the people of Jerusalem that the condition of their wicked hearts (emotions) is because of their undisciplined and unplanned thinking! Proverbs 21:5 gives us the cure. *"The thoughts of the diligent tend only to plenteousness."* A diligent man takes careful oversight of his thoughts. He is not lax. He plans what to think about and carries out that plan.

You will either plan what to think about each day, or you will fall victim to whatever mental fodder this world provides. Your eye gates and ear gates are constantly accosted by evil. The undisciplined, unplanned mind falls easy prey to whatever wickedness wanders in.

Replace evil thoughts with Bible meditations. The way to win the victory over wicked thinking is through Bible meditation.

Psalms 1:1-3 Blessed is the man that walketh not in the counsel of the ungodly, nor standeth in the way of sinners, nor sitteth in the seat of the scornful. But his delight is in the law of the LORD; and in his law doth he meditate day and night. And he shall be like a tree planted by the rivers of water, that bringeth forth his fruit in his season; his leaf also shall not wither; and whatsoever he doeth shall prosper.

Many of you young men have memorized Psalms chapter one. Its verses are so familiar that I am afraid you may have overlooked their promises. Bible meditation is essential to surviving the attacks of the Devil upon your mind. Nothing is more powerful than the Word of God! Jesus defeated Satan's temptations by quoting the Bible. If your mind is assaulted with evil thoughts, then you must discipline your thoughts on the Word of God. Psalms chapter one promises strength, life, fruit, health, and prosperity to the young man who will do so!

As you spend time each morning reading your Bible, it is essential that you choose out verses to jot down and carry with you throughout the day. Use a 3x5 card. Pull it out when needed and focus your mind on memorizing and meditating on those verses.

Replace worldly thinking with Christ thoughts. The more you study Christ, and meditate on His word, the more you will acquire His mind.

Phil 2:5 Let this mind be in you, which was also in Christ Jesus:
Romans 12:1-2 I beseech you therefore, brethren, by the mercies of God, that ye present your bodies a living sacrifice, holy, acceptable unto God, which is your reasonable service. And be not conformed to this world: but be ye transformed by the renewing of your mind, that ye may prove what is that good, and acceptable, and perfect, will of God.

The mind of Christ is characterized in Philippians, as one of humility and service — a mind fixed on fulfilling the will of His Father. The worldly mind set is just the opposite. It focuses on self and sin with little regard for eternity. You have to choose how you are going to think about each situation you face today. You can choose a Christ perspective or a worldly perspective. But remember, you win or lose the battle by how you choose! You also decide between boyhood and manhood.

Reputable Living
"In all things showing thyself a pattern of good works...."

The second of the four masculine disciplines is reputable living. Your life as a young man should show a pattern of good works. Every young man needs to stay busy. Many parents have filled their boys' lives with activity, but little of that activity could be described as "good works". Busyness can be vanity. It can be empty of anything meaningful and good. If someone were to pattern your life, they should see consistent activity that requires manly strength, and accomplishes something good for others and for eternity.

1 Thessalonians 5:22 Abstain from all appearance of evil.
Romans 14:16 Let not then your good be evil spoken of:

The way to keep a good reputation is to be very careful that your activities be pure in their appearance. The command of God is not just to abstain from evil, but to abstain from anything that might appear evil.

Schedule on a regular basis some good work that you can perform for your church, for your community, or for someone in need. Idleness is still the devil's workshop! Build a reputation of good works.

Pure Convictions
...in doctrine showing uncorruptness, gravity, sincerity....

Sound doctrine produces sound Christians. The word *sound* in the Bible is defined as *healthy*. Healthy doctrine produces healthy Christians. Corrupt doctrine will corrupt a Christian.

Every young man should spend time reading and studying the Bible for himself. But before forming convictions, he should spend time conversing with aged, godly men. This protects you from adopting beliefs that are corrupt, and that lack gravity (proven and honest) and sincerity (genuineness).

One man once said, "If it's new, it's not Bible, and if it's Bible, it's not new!" Often times young men get in trouble by chasing new, unproven beliefs. Aged, godly men whose lives are sound and proven are great sounding boards as you hone your convictions.

Excellent Speech
Sound speech, that cannot be condemned...

Men will judge you by what comes out of your mouth. Excellent speech is almost extinct among young men. This means if you are willing to work at developing it, you will be regarded as both wise and mature beyond your years.

Below are the *Ten Laws of Excellent Speech*. Discipline yourself not to speak if, in doing so, you would break one of these laws.

Law #1 — Speak Sparingly
Proverbs 17:27 He that hath knowledge spareth his words...
Proverbs10:19 In the multitude of words there wanteth not sin: but he that refraineth his lips is wise.

Notice that the Bible warns us that in a multitude of words, there wanteth not sin. Wanteth means lacketh. In a multitude of words there lacketh not sin! Idle, unplanned conversations always deteriorate into gossip. *Always.* Young man, learn to conserve your words. Spend more time listening than talking.

Law#2 — Speak Only After Thinking
Proverbs 29:20 Seest thou a man that is hasty in his words? there is more hope of a fool than of him.
James 1:19 Wherefore, my beloved brethren, let every man be swift to hear, slow to speak, slow to wrath:

Learn to be slow to speak. Most of the things you will regret saying are things you would not have said if you would have taken some time to their impact.

Law # 3 — Speak Honestly
Ephesians 4:25 Wherefore putting away lying, speak every man truth with his neighbour: for we are members one of another.
Proverbs 12:17 He that speaketh truth showeth forth righteousness: but a false witness deceit.

I am shocked at how many young men are habitual liars. Treat the truth sacredly. If you develop a reputation for dishonesty, no real man will trust you — or respect you.

Law #4 — Speak With Grace
Colossians 4:6 Let your speech be alway with grace, seasoned with salt, that ye may know how ye ought to answer every man.

Yes, speak the truth, but not everything that is true should be spoken. Grace is defined as "unmerited favor". Grace is likened to salt,

42

and salt is a preservative that prevents corruption. Your words should protect others, not destroy them. Let the golden rule guide you. Never speak an unkind truth.

Law #5 — Speak Only Acceptable Words
Psalms 19:14 Let the words of my mouth, and the meditation of my heart, be acceptable in thy sight, O LORD, my strength, and my redeemer.

Always ask yourself this question, "Is what I am about to say acceptable in the sight of God?" This discipline will eliminate from your vocabulary anything crude, vulgar, perverse, or questionable.

Law #6 — Speak Appropriately
Proverbs 25:11 A word fitly spoken is like apples of gold in pictures of silver.

I love the phrase, *"fitly spoken"*. Sometimes we say something that needs to be said, but we do not do it at a fitting time or in a fitting manner. An appropriate statement is a work of art when it is well-crafted and properly presented.

Law #7 — Speak Respectfully
1 Timothy 5:1-2 Rebuke not an elder, but entreat him as a father; and the younger men as brethren; The elder women as mothers; the younger as sisters, with all purity.

Always consider your tone when addressing people, especially your elders. You *entreat* an elder when you approach him or her with proper respect. Guard your attitude and never speak disrespectfully.

Law #8 — Never Speak Evil of Another Person
James 4:11 Speak not evil one of another, brethren.
Titus 3:1-2 ...speak evil of no man, to be no brawlers, but gentle, showing all meekness unto all men.

Don't purposefully say anything that is designed to defame someone. Gossip is a wicked, vile and evil sin. Never spread harmful and hurtful stories about anyone. Ever!

Law #9 — Never Praise Yourself

Proverbs 27:2 Let another man praise thee, and not thine own mouth; a stranger, and not thine own lips.

Nothing turns people off faster than a braggart. Be of a humble mind and spirit, and praise others instead of yourself.

Law #10 — Speak the Gospel Boldly

Romans 1:16 For I am not ashamed of the gospel of Christ: for it is the power of God unto salvation to every one that believeth; to the Jew first, and also to the Greek.

Always be a bold witness for Jesus Christ! One of the greatest privileges we have as a child of God is to share the wonderful Gospel story.

Boys speak too much, and usually without thinking. Immaturity is often dishonest or ungracious in what it says. Punks think vulgarity is amusing, disrespect is appropriate, gossiping is acceptable, and self-glorification is normal. Sadly, the same immature males are usually cowards when it comes to sharing the gospel.

Men are different. They say only what needs to be said, and then only after thinking it through. Masculinity speaks honestly, graciously, appropriately, and respectfully. Real men will not lower themselves to gossip or vulgarity, yet are always ready to speak a good word for the Lord Jesus Christ.

Excellent speech is the hallmark of excellent character. I dare you to yield your tongue as an instrument of righteousness. In doing so, you will achieve a level of maturity and discipline that will serve you well throughout your life.

(Author's Note: Each of the Ten Laws of Excellent Speech is dealt with in greater detail in my book, The Teenage Years of Jesus Christ available at www.stayinthecastle.com)

The four disciplines of Christian maturity — disciplined thinking, reputable living, pure convictions and excellent speech — are the gold standard of masculine character. Immaturity and carnality will always scorn these disciplines, deeming them nonessentials. Maturity and spirituality pursue these disciplines with laser focus.

TENET 14

Young men should master the three vital masculine skills.

*1 John 2:13-14 I write unto you, fathers, because ye have known him that is from the beginning. I write unto you, **young men**, because ye have overcome the wicked one. I write unto you, little children, because ye have known the Father. I have written unto you, fathers, because ye have known him that is from the beginning. I have written unto you, **young men**, because ye are strong, and the word of God abideth in you, and ye have overcome the wicked one.*

The apostle John writes to congratulate the young men for their success in mastering three vital masculine skills.

1. Overcoming Satanic attacks.
2. Developing spiritual strength.
3. Internalizing scriptural truth.

These three areas of Christian growth are interrelated and are a necessary part of Biblical masculinity. Boys succumb to Satanic attacks, men overcome them. Boys are spiritually weak, men are spiritually strong. Boys resist scriptural truth, men internalize scriptural truth.

The development of Biblical masculinity must include the development of these three masculine skills.

Overcoming Satanic Attacks
*"I write unto you, young men,
because ye have overcome the wicked one."*

Men were made to war. Most of the time, we foolishly fight each other, forgetting the real battle has and always will be a spiritual one.

Nothing is more satisfying than facing a direct Satanic assault and winning. Too many young men, when tempted by Satan, fold like a lawn chair! Most do so, not because they do not want to win, but because they have not mastered the art of spiritual warfare.

Spiritual armor is required to win a spiritual battle.

Ephesians 6:10-18 Finally, my brethren, be strong in the Lord, and in the power of his might. Put on the whole armour of God, that ye may be able to stand against the wiles of the devil. For we wrestle not against flesh and blood, but against principalities, against powers, against the rulers of the darkness of this world, against spiritual wickedness in high places. Wherefore take unto you the whole armour of God, that ye may be able to withstand in the evil day, and having done all, to stand. Stand therefore, having your loins girt about with truth, and having on the breastplate of righteousness; And your feet shod with the preparation of the gospel of peace; Above all, taking the shield of faith, wherewith ye shall be able to quench all the fiery darts of the wicked. And take the helmet of salvation, and the sword of the Spirit, which is the word of God: Praying always with all prayer and supplication in the Spirit....

This armor is specifically given to enable you to "stand against the wiles of the devil". The armor of God is necessary for you to "withstand in the evil day." Young man, this is not optional. Without this armor you have NO CHANCE to win a confrontation against the invisible, Satanic forces that WILL regularly accost you. Study carefully these seven essential virtues.

1. **Truth** — *Stand therefore, having your loins girt about with truth.* If you are a liar, you have no chance against the devil. You must commit yourself to truthfulness. The telling of a lie opens a Satanic door into your life. Notice what Jesus said concerning lying in John 8:44, *"Ye are of your father the devil, and the lusts of your father ye will do. He was a murderer from the beginning, and abode not in the truth, because there is no truth in him. When he*

46

speaketh a lie, he speaketh of his own: for he is a liar, and the father of it." If you tell a lie, the devil fathered it. You literally have to interact with the devil to lie. Lying puts at risk your morality. Honesty guards your loins — protects your purity. Immorality and dishonesty always go hand in hand. *Always!* Every young person who prematurely loses their purity lied their way into immorality. Being honest with God, with yourself, and with those in authority over you will protect you from the scarlet sin.

2. **Righteousness** — A breastplate protects your heart. A commitment to do right is an essential virtue in overcoming a Satanic attack. You must predetermine to do right. Choosing right BEFORE the temptation is much better than trying to choose right DURING a temptation. Make a heart commitment to do right!

3. **Witnessing** — Your feet must be "shod with the preparation of the gospel of peace". What that means is that everywhere you walk, you should be prepared to share by both life and lip the Gospel of the Lord Jesus Christ. Jesus attached the promise of both His presence and His protection to those engaged in fulfilling the Great Commission (Mat 28:18-20). Enlist in a soul winning ministry of your local church. Regularly witness in all arenas of your life. This will protect your feet and keep you on the right path.

4. **Faith** — This "shield" is the "above all" piece of armor. Faith obeys when it does not understand, obeys when it cannot see why, and obeys when it cannot see a benefit. It is a steadfast, unwavering reliance upon God and a whole-hearted commitment to serve God no matter the outcome. This virtue provides you with a shield able to *"quench all the fiery darts of the wicked."*

5. **Salvation** — This helmet protects your mind. You must be able to find on the timeline of your life a point where you KNOW you were saved. Many a young man quietly lives his life plagued with doubts about his salvation. Doubting distracts you in battle. If you are going through this, talk to a trusted older Christian and settle this once and for all. A know-so salvation protects your mind.

6. **The Word of God** — The Bible is your sword. A young man who is unskilled in its usage is unfit for battle. You need to read *and* study the Word of God. The mastery of this weapon will allow you

to win against the devil. Jesus gave us the example of its effectiveness as He battled Satan in the wilderness. You cannot win against the devil without the Scriptures.

7. **Prayer** — A prayerless young man is a victim waiting to happen. Put on the armor, then kneel humbly before your Maker.

Spiritual action is necessary to win a spiritual battle.

When you realize that you are under a direct Satanic attack, you need to have an immediate plan of action. This is not a time for confusion or hesitancy. This plan of action is based on the following Bible verses. Study these verses, then commit to heart the action plan.

Luke 10:17 And the seventy returned again with joy, saying, Lord, even the devils are subject unto us through thy name.

Jude 1:9 Yet Michael the archangel, when contending with the devil he disputed about the body of Moses, durst not bring against him a railing accusation, but said, The Lord rebuke thee.

Luke 4:8 And Jesus answered and said unto him, Get thee behind me, Satan: for it is written, Thou shalt worship the Lord thy God, and him only shalt thou serve.

Rev 12:9-11 And the great dragon was cast out, that old serpent, called the Devil, and Satan, which deceiveth the whole world: he was cast out into the earth, and his angels were cast out with him. And I heard a loud voice saying in heaven, Now is come salvation, and strength, and the kingdom of our God, and the power of his Christ: for the accuser of our brethren is cast down, which accused them before our God day and night. And they overcame him by the blood of the Lamb, and by the word of their testimony; and they loved not their lives unto the death.

How are you to respond to a Satanic attack? You respond with a Bible-based, well planned and practiced counter-attack!

1. **Rebuke Satan in Jesus' name.** Jesus' disciples found out that *"even the devils are subject unto us through thy name."* Michael

the archangel used the Lord's name to win a battle against the devil. There is power in the name of JESUS! Verbally rebuke Satan in the name of Jesus when you come under Satanic attack.

2. **Resist Satan by quoting appropriate Scripture.** I recommend that every young man have three verses committed to memory for the express purpose of spiritual warfare: ***Luke 4:8***, *"Get thee behind me: for it is written, Thou shalt worship the Lord thy God, and him only shalt thou serve.* ***James 4:7*** *"Submit yourselves therefore to God. Resist the devil, and he will flee from you."* ***Phil 4:13*** *"I can do all things through Christ which strengtheneth me."* We learn from the example of Christ to defeat Satanic attacks by quoting scripture. Use the Sword of the Spirit!

3. **Remind Satan of the blood of Christ.** Revelation chapter 12 tells us that the saints of God overcame the old serpent *"by the blood of the Lamb"*. Verbally remind Satan of what happened on Calvary! The perfect sacrifice of Christ defeated Satan forever. There is power in the BLOOD!

4. **Respond with an evangelistic counter attack!** Again, in Revelation 12:11, Satan was overcome by *"...the word of their testimonies"*. The saints of God got on the offensive! Counter every Satanic attack with renewed vigor in sharing your testimony with others. Put HIM on the defensive! Satanic attacks *against you* should always result in increased evangelistic activity *by you*.

5. **Refuse to surrender no matter what.** Notice the entirety of ***Revelation 12:11***: *"And they overcame him by the blood of the Lamb, and by the word of their testimony; and they loved not their lives unto the death."* The saints that overcame Satan "loved not their lives unto the death". They were all in! The early Christians of Acts were near invincible because they possessed a martyr's mentality! Live or die, they were going to serve God. Boys do things that are convenient; men do their duty. ***Philippians 1:20-21***, *"According to my earnest expectation and my hope, that in nothing I shall be ashamed, but that with all boldness, as always, so now also Christ shall be magnified in my body, whether it be by life, or by death. For to me to live is Christ, and to die is gain."*

49

Practice this five-step plan of action! The next time Satan attacks, you can experience victory through Christ's name, His shed blood, His Holy Word, an aggressive counter-attack, and a manly resolve to do right, no matter the cost!

Developing Spiritual Strength

"I have written unto you, young men, because ye are strong..."

Two births are necessary for us to enter the kingdom of heaven — the water (physical) birth and the Spirit (spiritual) rebirth. We are born sinners, "dead in trespasses and sins". Upon salvation, the Holy Spirit enters into that man and regenerates that lost man's dead spirit. His spirit is born again by the Holy Spirit and becomes a new creature in Christ!

*John 3:5-7 Jesus answered, Verily, verily, I say unto thee, Except a man be born of water and of the Spirit, he cannot enter into the kingdom of God. That which is born of the flesh is flesh; **and that which is born of the Spirit is spirit**. Marvel not that I said unto thee, Ye must be born again.*

Our new born spirit needs to grow in strength. A "spiritual" Christian, simply put, is a Christian whose born again spirit is empowered by the Holy Spirit to control and discipline their soul and body. A carnal Christian, by contrast, is a Christian whose flesh takes the lead, influencing the man's soul (mind, heart & will) away from the leading of the Holy Spirit. This carnal Christian is spiritually weak, and sadly unproductive for God.

The Bible gives us specific instruction on how to strengthen our new born spirit. It does not happen by accident. Young man, let me ask you straight out, are you spiritually strong or are you spiritually weak? Which part of you is running your life — your flesh, or your Holy Spirit-controlled, reborn spirit?

Prayer Strengthens the Spirit

Matthew 26:41 Watch and pray, that ye enter not into temptation: the spirit indeed is willing, but the flesh is weak.

Isaiah 40:31 But they that wait upon the LORD shall renew their strength; they shall mount up with wings as eagles; they shall run, and not be weary; and they shall walk, and not faint.

Our spirit gains strength when we spend time at the throne of grace. God's throne is our spiritual refueling station. In His presence is fullness of joy! Prayerlessness weakens the spirit.

The Word of God Strengthens the Spirit
John 6:63 It is the spirit that quickeneth; the flesh profiteth nothing: the words that I speak unto you, they are spirit, and they are life.
Hebrews 4:12-13 For the word of God is quick, and powerful, and sharper than any twoedged sword, piercing even to the dividing asunder of soul and spirit, and of the joints and marrow, and is a discerner of the thoughts and intents of the heart. Neither is there any creature that is not manifest in his sight: but all things are naked and opened unto the eyes of him with whom we have to do.

The Word of God is food for our spirit. It is the "milk", the "manna", the "strong meat" we need for daily strength. Without it, we quickly become spiritually weak.

Psalms, Hymns and Spiritual Songs Strengthen the Spirit
Ephesians 5:18-19 And be not drunk with wine, wherein is excess; but be filled with the Spirit; Speaking to yourselves in psalms and hymns and spiritual songs, singing and making melody in your heart to the Lord;
Colossians 3:16 Let the word of Christ dwell in you richly in all wisdom; teaching and admonishing one another in psalms and hymns and spiritual songs, singing with grace in your hearts to the Lord.

By definition, "spiritual songs" are songs that target and strengthen your reborn spirit. The world's music, with its carnal beat and sinful message, wears down your spirit and strengthens your flesh.

Denying the Flesh Strengthens the Spirit
Galatians 5:17-18 For the flesh lusteth against the Spirit, and the Spirit against the flesh: and these are contrary the one to the other: so that ye cannot do the things that ye would...

Romans 13:14 But put ye on the Lord Jesus Christ, and make not provision for the flesh, to fulfil the lusts thereof.

Young man, you will never be spiritually strong as long as you make provision for your flesh. Hollywood movies, worldly music, filthy websites, carnal friends, inappropriate reading material, a wandering, lustful eye — they are all contrary to spiritual growth and development.

Your new born spirit will only grow strong through prayer, consumption of the Word of God, spiritual music, and self-denial. Choose you this day whom you will serve — your flesh, or your Spirit-controlled spirit.

Internalizing Scriptural Truth
"I have written unto you, young men, because ...
the word of God abideth in you..."

John congratulated young men because the "word of God abideth in you". Bible truth must be internalized. As a young man, it is time to make the Word of God a part of who you are. Some men read the Bible, few men internalize it. The word "abideth" means *to stay, continue, dwell, endure, be present, or remain.* When the Word of God is sown from the pulpit, let your heart be fertile soil where Bible principles can find root, grow and produce fruit in your life.

Every time you read the Bible, latch on to something and let it become a part of you, and you a part of it. Ask God to give you one great truth from every sermon you hear, then become that truth. Live it from that day forward. Don't just be a *hearer*, but be a *doer* of the word. Secure truth and integrate it into your character.

Some of you already know a lot of Bible — facts, stories, names, places, events, and even truths. Good. Awesome. But understand this, God is not impressed with how much Bible you *know*, he is impressed by how much Bible you *live*.

Christian boys know the Bible. Christian men live the Bible.

Review this chapter. Remember, you advance your spiritual masculinity by mastering three vital spiritual skills — overcoming Satanic attacks, developing spiritual strength, and internalizing scriptural truth.

TENET 15

Young men must learn to face and defeat giants.

*1 Samuel 17:42-50 And when the Philistine looked about, and saw David, he disdained him: for **he was but a youth**, and ruddy, and of a fair countenance. And the Philistine said unto David, Am I a dog, that thou comest to me with staves? And the Philistine cursed David by his gods. And the Philistine said to David, Come to me, and I will give thy flesh unto the fowls of the air, and to the beasts of the field. Then said David to the Philistine, Thou comest to me with a sword, and with a spear, and with a shield: but I come to thee in the name of the LORD of hosts, the God of the armies of Israel, whom thou hast defied. This day will the LORD deliver thee into mine hand; and I will smite thee, and take thine head from thee; and I will give the carcases of the host of the Philistines this day unto the fowls of the air, and to the wild beasts of the earth; that all the earth may know that there is a God in Israel. And all this assembly shall know that the LORD saveth not with sword and spear: for the battle is the Lord's, and he will give you into our hands. And it came to pass, when the Philistine arose, and came and drew nigh to meet David, that David hasted, and ran toward the army to meet the Philistine. And David put his hand in his bag, and took thence a stone, and slang it, and smote the Philistine in his forehead, that the stone sunk into his forehead; and he fell upon his face to the earth. So David prevailed over the Philistine with a sling and with a stone, and smote the Philistine, and slew him;*

Young men in Israel had to be twenty years of age in order to go to war (Numbers 1:3). David was not allowed to join Saul's army, but instead stayed home and tended the sheep. He was on the battlefield that day when Goliath presented himself because his father had sent him to take food to his brothers. In this story, David was still a teenager, yet he was about to take a huge step into manhood.

The transitioning from boyhood to manhood will involve some epic battles. Many of these battles will be fought within you — a few without. Reread the battle story, and then let's learn from David.

David fought this battle in God's strength and for God's glory. Only fight battles that will provide God glory. Spiritual immaturity fights in defense of one's pride, spiritual maturity fights for the glory of God. Always defend God's name, God's people and God's glory.

David was willing to die for a cause! A boy lives for himself. A man lives for a cause and, if necessary, is willing to die for that cause. For the Christian young man, the cause of Christ should reign supreme. Our King is worth living for, fighting for, and if necessary dying for!

David did not run from Goliath, he ran to meet him. Avoiding a confrontation with a giant only postpones the conflict. Our giants — those things that rise up inside of us or before us and seek to bring dishonor to the Lord — sooner or later must be faced down.

David was confident to face this giant, because of previous private victories. When King Saul questioned David about his youthfulness and battle readiness, David told the story of a lion and a bear he defeated while all alone, guarding his father's sheep. If you will not exercise the courage to win private victories, you will probably struggle with public battles.

David used a simple but proven weapon. He turned down King Saul's weapon and armor. David chose to face Goliath with a sling, five stones, and great faith in God. No matter how young you are, how inexperienced in warfare, or how simple your weapons, you can win against a giant if you fight in the name of the Lord!

David did not just knock down the giant, he cut off his head. David finished the job. Too many times a young man wins the battle but loses the war. A giant must be destroyed.

In the next chapter, I will introduce you to five giants that will challenge you greatly in your youth — five giants that need to be slain.

TENET 16

Young men must learn that there are sins linked to youthfulness that will cause them great struggles.

*Job 20:11 His bones are full of **the sin of his youth**, which shall lie down with him in the dust.*

*Job 13:26 For thou writest bitter things against me, and makest me to possess **the iniquities of my youth**.*

*Psalms 25:7 Remember not **the sins of my youth**, nor my transgressions: according to thy mercy remember thou me for thy goodness' sake, O LORD.*

Most young Christian boys do fairly well spiritually, until they reach puberty. As you leave boyhood and grow physically into manhood, you will begin to notice significant changes in your body. God is preparing you and equipping you to reproduce — to be able to have children of your own someday.

These physical changes will also become your giants.

Puberty occurs years before it is wise or acceptable to marry a wife. God created us this way for a reason. As a young man, God wants you to know (to understand, to learn) how to possess your body in sanctification and honor. God does not ask you to do something you are not able to do with His help.

1 Thes 4:3-5 For this is the will of God, even your sanctification, that ye should abstain from fornication: That every one of you should know how to possess his vessel in sanctification and honour; Not in the lust of concupiscence, even as the Gentiles which know not God:

Young man, I will be honest with you — the subject of personal purity during your youth is one that is only addressed in general terms. However, ignoring the problem as if it doesn't exist is not helping young men. God's Word can help equip you to fight and win this battle against your own flesh. *It is the will of God that you abstain from fornication. Abstain means to hold oneself off, to refrain.* A Christian young man has all of the same physical reproductive drives as a lost man, but because he is a Christian, he must choose to discipline himself — to hold off on satisfying those desires until marriage, and then only within his marriage relationship.

To do this, you will need five smooth stones and a weapon to sling them. You are going to have to knock down five giants. You will also need a sword, so bring it along. The battle isn't over until you cut off their heads.

The Five Giants of Gath

Egypt in the Bible always represents the world. The land of the Philistines represents the flesh. Goliath and his four brothers were Philistines. There are five giants of the flesh that you will have to slay in your young man years, or they very well may slay you.

One man once said, "Puberty does not come with an instruction manual." Well, actually it does. The Bible helps a young man understand how to manage the physical changes he is facing, while still possessing his body in sanctification and honor.

*Colossians 3: 5-6, Mortify therefore your members which are upon the earth; **fornication, uncleanness, inordinate affection, evil concupiscence, and covetousness**, which is idolatry: For which things' sake the wrath of God cometh on the children of disobedience:*

Remember, the word mortify means to kill. You do not make excuses for these sins, you kill them. You do not make peace with them, make provision for them, or make place for them — you mortify them. You do not just knock them down, you cut off their heads. Now, let's kill some giants!

The Giant of Fornication

The word *fornication* found in I Thessalonians 4:3 is an umbrella word that covers all forms of mental or physical activity that encourages sexual activity *before* or *outside* of a married relationship.

Your first line of defense in fighting the battle for mental and physical purity is to accept God's definition of fornication, and His mandate to abstain from fornication.

1 Thes 4:3-4 For this is the will of God, even your sanctification, that ye should abstain from fornication: That every one of you should know how to possess his vessel in sanctification and honour;

Satan wants to convince you that there are some forms of mental or physical sexual activity that are acceptable. He will even go so far as to lie to you and try to convince you that some forms are normal, even healthy! He will tell you lies like, "Everyone does it." and "Self -abuse is better than becoming sexually active with a girl." A young man who surrenders to the quiet giant of secret lust is setting himself up for destruction.

Matthew 5:27-28 Ye have heard that it was said by them of old time, Thou shalt not commit adultery: But I say unto you, That who-soever looketh on a woman to lust after her hath committed adultery with her already in his heart.

If you are going to win this battle, you must define fornication the same way God does in His Word. Again, fornication is ANY mental or physical activity that encourages sexual activity before or outside of the marriage relationship. The way you cut off the head of this giant is to allow no redefining of who he is and what he stands for. Make "no provision for the flesh, to fulfill the lust thereof" (Romans 13:14).

The Giant of Uncleanness

Uncleanness is defined as lewd, impure or unclean behavior. The *Giant of Fornication* tries to get you to redefine improper behavior as proper. Then the *Giant of Uncleanness* encourages you to participate in improper behavior. The first giant tells you it's acceptable, the second encourages its activity.

God tells you to be honorable. God tells you to sanctify your body. God tells you to flee fornication.

1 Corinthians 6:18-20 Flee fornication. Every sin that a man doeth is without the body; but he that committeth fornication sinneth against his own body. What? know ye not that your body is the temple of the Holy Ghost which is in you, which ye have of God, and ye are not your own? For ye are bought with a price: therefore glorify God in your body, and in your spirit, which are God's.

No young man should participate in any form of self-abuse or sexual activity before marriage. None! Your body is the temple of the Holy Spirit. You have been bought with a price. Your duty is to glorify God in your body, and in your spirit, which are HIS.

The Giant of Inordinate Affection

When a young man fails to slay the first two giants, then they are joined by a third — the *Giant of Inordinate Affection*.

Justifying or redefining fornication will lead to participation in some form of secret fornication. What may seem harmless and exciting begins to affect the condition of your heart!

What is inordinate affection? Inordinate affection is a sin of the heart. It is an inner grief or suffering over an unrealized passion; a sympathy for self, a martyr's mentality, a sadness of soul because of something strongly longed for but temporarily denied.

The *Giant of Fornication* wants you to redefine improper behavior as proper. The *Giant of Uncleanness* convinces you to participate in some level of improper behavior. The *Giant of Inordinate Affection* stirs up feelings of self-pity and sadness because that which you constantly fantasize about you cannot properly have.

This *Giant of Inordinate Affection* complains to your heart about your parent's rules. He stirs hostile emotions against any teaching about restraint or proper courtship guidelines. He encourages you to roll around in self pity and sadness, and convinces you that you are being mistreated and deprived.

Again, it is a sin of the heart. Improper definition led to improper conduct which stirs improper attitudes toward authority and rules. The *Giant of Inordinate Affection* whispers constantly, "Poor you. It's not fair. You'll never be happy. Why don't people just leave you alone and let you follow your heart. It's none of their business. You should be able to have what you want."

Inordinate affection always produces strong feelings of discontent. You begin to spend much time wallowing in self-pity because that which God intended for you to experience later, you have insisted on stirring up now. Unclean actions produce improper passions. You begin to become wrong in your heart, and that opens you up for an attack by the next giant.

The Giant of Evil Concupiscence

Inordinate affection, if not properly dealt with leads to evil concupiscence. This giant is a monster. Evil concupiscence is a depraved longing for what is forbidden by God. It is an evil, harmful, noisome and wicked desire for that which God clearly says is off limits. Self-pity now leads to self-indulgence. *Inordinate Affection* pollutes the heart and then *Evil Concupiscence* pollutes the mind.

This giant focuses a young man's thought processes constantly on the lust of his flesh. He no longer views Christian young ladies as "sisters, with all purity" (I Timothy 5:2) but as sexual objects to fantasize about. This unholy mindset feeds on debauchery.

What happened? If you are here, how did you get here? How do you get help?

You got here by first redefining improper behavior as proper, then engaging in unclean behavior as if it were normal. This always leads to self-pity and sadness because of desires stirred that cannot be properly satisfied. As a result you are plagued with discontentment and bitterness!

Now enters the *Giant of Evil Concupiscence* who encourages self-indulgence.

If you are here, you need to go back and kill the giants in the proper order. Slay your improper defining of fornication. Then slay your unclean actions. Then slay your self-pity and bitterness. Then slay your perverted musings.

If you do not, the next giant will destroy your life.

The Giant of Covetousness
(which is idolatry)

Colossians 3: 5-6, Mortify therefore your members which are upon the earth; **fornication, uncleanness, inordinate affection, evil concupiscence, and covetousness**, *which is idolatry: For which things' sake the wrath of God cometh on the children of disobedience:*

This last giant is the creation of the other four. He stands, demanding that you satisfy the unholy greed you have created. *Covetousness* demands to be served at any cost. He badgers you into satisfying your desires. He demands servitude and cares not what unscrupulous means (fraud, extortion, defrauding, deceit, manipulation, even force) you use.

The *Giant of Covetousness* wants to become your god! He wants you to bring him sacrifices. He wants you to sacrifice to him your decency, your future, God's perfect will, your future wife and children, your calling, your relationship with Godly authorities, your common sense and self-esteem. He is a wicked and selfish anti-Christ. And MANY young Christian men have been slain at his feet!

Covetousness is defined as desiring something that does not belong to you. In this context, it is specifically addressing the lusts of the flesh.

A fleshly young man says, "I want that man's wife."

"I want that girl who is some other man's future wife."

"I want what God says is not yet mine to have."

"I want that ungodly young lady."

"I want NOW what God has reserved for LATER!"

"I WILL have a girlfriend no matter what authority says"

"I want self-indulgence and self-satisfaction at any cost!"

A young man who gets to this point is an easy victim for the devil. This young man has turned fleshly lusts into an idol. He worships at its feet, serves it whole heartedly, and has become a slave to its every whim. This young man is on the road to becoming a reprobate.

Can this last giant be slain? Absolutely. Yes, there is hope in God! I have counseled with young men who had become slaves to these giants. They were living in chains of bondage, living on the devil's leash, fools on display for the world to see. I have also seen God set them free. But they had to be willing to kill the giants.

Psalms 119:9-11 Wherewithal shall a young man cleanse his way? by taking heed thereto according to thy word. With my whole heart have I sought thee: O let me not wander from thy commandments. Thy word have I hid in mine heart, that I might not sin against thee.

Let's line up the five giants of the flesh — and then let's understand how to slay them!

Fornication — Understand that ALL activity (mental or physical) that leads to ANY sexual activity is viewed by God as the sin of fornication. Refuse to let the devil redefine anything related to this area of your life as acceptable! Protect your eye-gates and your ear-gates from anything that could defraud you. Separate yourself from those who encourage you to redefine what God has condemned!

Uncleanness — Mortify ALL mental and physical sexual activity. This battle can be won! Bible memorization and meditation is essential for a young man to cleanse his way.

Inordinate Affection — Repent of the heart-sin of self-pity! God is NOT unreasonable in asking you to follow the timeline of His will. Everything that is pure and good awaits you down the road, in a proper and blessed relationship with the woman God has created for you. Until then, commit yourself to possess your body in sanctification and honor.

Evil Concupiscence — Guard your mind! Train yourself to look away from that which stirs up fleshly lusts. Build accountability into your life. Learn to focus on that which is holy and right.

Covetousness — Make a determined decision of your will to refuse to lust after that which does not belong to you. Pray daily for the young lady God has somewhere in your future. Expend your mental and physical energies on becoming a young man worthy of one day accepting a virtuous young lady to be your wife.

Count the Cost

Satan will waste no time in trying to convince you that what I have covered in this chapter is of no consequence. He will tell you there exists no long term consequences to participating in secret, immoral sins of your youth. He will tell you the five giants are not enemies to be slain, but companions and confidants to be courted.

Before you believe the lies of the devil, you might want to remind yourself of the consequences connected with the immoral life.

Proverbs 7:6-27 — *"For at the window of my house I looked through my casement, And beheld among the simple ones, I discerned among the youths, a young man void of understanding, Passing through the street near her corner; and he went the way to her house, In the twilight, in the evening, in the black and dark night: And, behold, there met him a woman with the attire of an harlot, and subtle of heart......With her much fair speech she caused him to yield, with the flattering of her lips she forced him. He goeth after her straightway, as an ox goeth to the slaughter, or as a fool to the correction of the stocks; Till a dart strike through his liver; as a bird hasteth to the snare, and knoweth not that it is for his life. Hearken unto me now therefore, O ye children, and attend to the words of my mouth. Let not thine heart decline to her ways, go not astray in her paths. For she hath cast down many wounded: yea, many strong men have been slain by her. Her house is the way to hell, going down to the chambers of death."*

Proverbs 6:27 *"Can a man take fire in his bosom, and his clothes not be burned?"*

TENET 17

A young man should practice chivalry.

*1 Timothy 5:1 Rebuke not an elder, but entreat him as a father; and the **younger men** as brethren; The elder women as mothers; the younger as sisters, with all purity. Honour widows that are widows indeed.*

Psalms 18:35 Thou hast also given me the shield of thy salvation: and thy right hand hath holden me up, and thy gentleness hath made me great.

Galatians 5:22-23 But the fruit of the Spirit is love, joy, peace, long-suffering, gentleness, goodness, faith, meekness, temperance: against such there is no law.

A good definition of chivalry is thus: *the combination of qualities expected of an ideal knight; courage, honor, courtesy, justice, and a readiness to help the weak; courteous behavior, especially that of a man towards a woman.*

Chivalry is the art of being a gentleman.

Part of becoming a man is learning the value of gentleness. A man who is secure in his masculinity has no problem extending to others proper courtesy and respect. Weak men bully others, striving to feel powerful by preying upon the weak. Real men are gentle toward others, displaying their strength by helping and defending the weak. Chivalry is a prerequisite to manhood.

Chivalry Towards Women

A real man conducts himself with honor towards women. In the first three verses of 1 Timothy, chapter 5, the Bible instructs young men to treat the elder women as mothers, the younger women as sisters with all purity, and to show special honor to widows. This gives us the basis of chivalry towards women.

You should treat every woman with great respect, courtesy and gentleness. Around women, your behavior should be beyond reproach. Never be crude, boorish, or disrespectful in the presence of a woman. Your words should be careful, kind, and pure. Common courtesies such as standing when a woman enters the room, holding open a door, giving up your seat, or allowing her to go first should be normal for any young man.

Chivalry towards ladies should be honed within your own family. Your grandmother, mother and sisters should be blessed to dwell in the presence of a gentleman. A young male who treats his female family members with disrespect and disdain is not a man, but an insecure little boy, no matter what his age.

Young ladies should feel safe, sacred, and special in your presence. You generate these feelings from them by the respect and regard you show towards them. Be kind but not flirtatious, helpful but not intrusive, and pure in your thoughts, words and actions.

Always be protective of ladies. Never mistreat a lady or allow anyone else to do so in your presence. A young man should be prepared to die in the protection of his wife, mother or sisters. Chivalry would allow for nothing less.

Chivalry protects the reputation of a lady. Again, the Bible instructs you to treat "the younger women as sisters, with all purity." A real man refuses to view women as sex objects. When addressing a lady, his words are appropriate, his eyes looking only at her eyes, and his mind, respectful and pure. By doing so, he not only protects her reputation, but also his own.

Every woman is somebody's grandmother, mother, wife, sister, or daughter. A gentleman understands this, and treats them with the same respect he would expect other men to treat his female family members.

Chivalry Towards Aged Men and Women

Always show great respect towards aged men and women. As

opportunity allows, do everything within your power to make their lives easier. Speak kindly, humbly and gently to senior citizens. Remember, age comes to us all, and what you sow in this area of your life, you will someday reap.

Every aged woman is your mother, and every aged man your father. This is how God wants you to consider them, for by doing so, you will treat them properly. Use your youthful strength and energy to their advantage.

Take the time to listen to aged men and women. Glean from them their life experiences and the knowledge and wisdom they have gained. Gift them your time and attention.

Cherish your grandparents. They are your link to another time and to the part of your family now buried and gone. Hear the stories of your heritage. Learn from them your history, and the history of your nation.

1 Timothy 5:3-8 Honour widows that are widows indeed. But if any widow have children or nephews, let them learn first to show piety at home, and to requite their parents: for that is good and acceptable before God...But if any provide not for his own, and specially for those of his own house, he hath denied the faith, and is worse than an infidel.

Widows are to receive special honor. The Bible places on every member of society the responsibility of caring for widows. This responsibility first starts at home. A family who will not care for their aged members is a family of infidels. A manly code of honor always includes respect and care towards the elderly.

Chivalry Towards Children

Matthew 18:1-6 At the same time came the disciples unto Jesus, saying, Who is the greatest in the kingdom of heaven? And Jesus called a little child unto him, and set him in the midst of them, And said, Verily I say unto you, Except ye be converted, and become as little children, ye shall not enter into the kingdom of heaven. Whosoever

*therefore shall humble himself as this little child, the same is great-
est in the kingdom of heaven. And whoso shall receive one such
little child in my name receiveth me. But whoso shall offend one of
these little ones which believe in me, it were better for him that a
millstone were hanged about his neck, and that he were drowned in
the depth of the sea.*

*Matthew 19:13-15 Then were there brought unto him little chil-
dren, that he should put his hands on them, and pray: and the disciples rebuked them. But Jesus said, Suffer little children, and forbid
them not, to come unto me: for of such is the kingdom of heaven.
And he laid his hands on them, and departed thence.*

The example of Christ is an example of chivalry towards children. He took time for them and was a blessing to them. He
warned of stern judgment upon those who would mistreat them. He
saw in them great potential. Jesus promised, "whoso shall receive
one such little child in my name receiveth me."

Chivalry protects the weak. It understands that children need
role models and mentors. A real man will always take the time to
invest in the life of a child. To do so is to invest in the future.

Young man, if your example in front of those younger than you
is a stumbling block to their proper development, Christ warns that
millstone justice awaits you! To lead a child astray by your wicked
example of immaturity and indecency is a crime against the weak,
against your nation, and against God. Take seriously your responsibility towards children, and take special care to bless the fatherless.

*James 1:27 Pure religion and undefiled before God and the Father
is this, To visit the fatherless and widows in their affliction, and to
keep himself unspotted from the world.*

Chivalry is a code of behavior — a code of conduct becoming a
Christian gentleman. That code includes courtesy and proper conduct towards all mankind, but especially towards ladies, the aged,
children, and anyone who is weak or in need.

TENET 18

A young man should marry in his youth, and should discover all of the pleasures of women through one woman — the wife of his youth.

*Proverbs 5:18-19 Let thy fountain be blessed: and rejoice with the wife of **thy youth**. Let her be as the loving hind and pleasant roe; let her breasts satisfy thee at all times; and be thou ravished always with her love.*

In the introduction of this booklet, I defined "young men" as males between the ages of 12 and 30. Obviously, this chapter is not directed at young men in the lower ages of this window. However, it should be an encouragement to young men of all ages. One of the greatest motivations for slaying the giants listed in chapter 16 is out of respect for the young lady that you will someday marry. A tragic and unfair inconsistency in our culture is the way we divide our view of immorality by gender. If a young lady loses her virginity, we look upon her as shamed, but if a young man loses his virginity, we seem to view this as less shameful. God doesn't! Young man, if you want to someday marry a pure young bride, then decide to be pure yourself.

Everything that you discover about women should be discovered through one woman — the wife of your youth. Marriages are self-destructing everywhere because of the immoral baggage being carried into these marriages by young men and young women who refused to live pure and holy in their youth. Short term indulgences cause long term consequences. Be patient, prepare and pray. All you desire is waiting up ahead, within the time frame of the perfect will of God.

Genesis 2:18-25 And the LORD God said, It is not good that the man should be alone; I will make him an help meet for him...And the LORD God caused a deep sleep to fall upon Adam, and he slept: and he took one of his ribs, and closed up the flesh instead thereof; And the rib, which the LORD God had taken from man, made he a woman, and brought her unto the man. And Adam said, This is now bone of my bones, and flesh of my flesh: she shall be called Woman, because she was taken out of Man. Therefore shall a man leave his father and his mother, and shall cleave unto his wife: and they shall be one flesh. And they were both naked, the man and his wife, and were not ashamed.

God has created someone specifically for you! Eve was made as the perfect complement to Adam. God has created an Eve for you.

A part of you is in that specific one created for you! This is an amazing thought! Part of Adam was used in the construction of Eve. I believe He has done the same for you.

You will never feel complete until God brings this person to you. Eve was Adam's completer. The two became one flesh. The feeling of incompleteness you battle is real. Satan will try to exploit this normal frustration by tempting you to run ahead of God's will and by offering you a counterfeit!

God will bring this person to you in His time. Be patient! God put Adam into a *"deep sleep"*, then woke him when it was time to present Eve. Ask God to do the same for you! A foolish boy spends his teen years pursuing girls; a wise young man spends his teen years preparing for the one God will one day bring to him.

Stay focused on finding and doing God's will. Along that path you will meet the one who will be your life partner. God created Adam, put him in the garden, and gave him responsibilities and rules. Adam focused on doing the will of God until God brought Eve to him. He did not leave the garden to seek after a woman! You were created to do something great for God! In His time, God will bring to a young man who whole-heartedly pursues His will, a completer, companion and lover who will help him in his life's calling.

TENET 19

Young men should understand the importance of bearing a yoke in their youth, and the danger of an unequal yoke.

*Proverbs 20:29 The glory of **young men** is their strength: and the beauty of old men is the grey head.*

What a wonderful thing when the strength of a young man is guided by the wisdom of an older man! The wise young man will yoke often with older men, providing him both a Godly example and sage advice.

*Lamentations 3:27 It is good for a man that he bear the yoke **in his youth**.*

God says a proper yoke is a good thing for a man in his youth! Most young men tout their need for freedom, and spew nonsense such as "I should be allowed to make my own mistakes." With that attitude, they will have no shortage of them!

Matthew 11:28-30 Come unto me, all ye that labour and are heavy laden, and I will give you rest. Take my yoke upon you, and learn of me; for I am meek and lowly in heart: and ye shall find rest unto your souls. For my yoke is easy, and my burden is light.

Jesus offers to each of us His yoke. A yoke takes the strength of two, and combines them into one. This gives us a measure of "rest" even though we are still laboring. It eliminates us becoming "heavy laden", or overwhelmed.

A yoke is also an instrument for learning. "Take my yoke upon you, and learn of me…" Young, unbroken oxen were often yoked with older, experienced oxen. The young learned how to do the work by spending time yoked to experience. Young man, yoke up with Christ!

The ultimate goal of the Christian life is to be like Jesus. Time spent studying the Savior is a wise investment.

Jesus goes on to say, "For my yoke is easy, and my burden is light." Every young man yokes up with someone or something! Sin is a cruel taskmaster. The devil's yoke is neither easy or light. Nor is it ever as easy to get off as it was to get on! Be wise. Many a young man, who was determined to "get free" of the yoke of a Christian upbringing, found themselves slaves to sin and the world.

2 Corinthians 6:14-7:1 Be ye not unequally yoked together with unbelievers: for what fellowship hath righteousness with unrighteousness? and what communion hath light with darkness? And what concord hath Christ with Belial? or what part hath he that believeth with an infidel? And what agreement hath the temple of God with idols? for ye are the temple of the living God; as God hath said, I will dwell in them, and walk in them; and I will be their God, and they shall be my people. Wherefore come out from among them, and be ye separate, saith the Lord, and touch not the unclean thing; and I will receive you, And will be a Father unto you, and ye shall be my sons and daughters, saith the Lord Almighty. Having therefore these promises, dearly beloved, let us cleanse ourselves from all filthiness of the flesh and spirit, perfecting holiness in the fear of God.

Never yoke up with unbelievers, unrighteousness, darkness, Belial, infidels, or idolatry. Choose instead to yoke together with believers, righteousness, light, Christ, truth, and the house of God. The yoke you choose determines your destiny!

Never apologize for your separatist stand. We are to come out from among them and be separate. A special Father/son kinship and resemblance results from holy living. Young man, cleanse yourself from all filthiness of the flesh and spirit. Work at perfecting holiness in the fear of God. Choose carefully your yokes! Some will try to sell you on the idea of a "worldly Christianity". Remember, if you have to become like the world to "reach" the world, you have not reached the world, the world has reached you!

TENET 20

Young men should counter the natural inclination of older men to undervalue their youthfulness by showing stellar character in six important areas.

*1 Timothy 4:12 Let no man despise **thy youth**; but be thou an example of the believers, in word, in conversation, in charity, in spirit, in faith, in purity.*

Here is a fact — older men sometimes undervalue and underestimate the importance and potential of young men. They probably shouldn't, but they do. Paul warned young Timothy of this danger. He also placed on this young man the responsibility of living in such a way as to gain the respect of his elders.

Right now, you have a reputation among godly adults. Adults watch young people. They base their assessment of you by examining six areas of your life. In these six areas, you are commanded by God to be an example of what a believer is supposed to be: in word, in conversation, in charity, in spirit, in faith, in purity.

Gaining the Respect of Men

Adults respect excellent speech. Words are a window to your soul, a spilling out of the abundance of your heart. They reveal to men who you really are. Review the *"Ten Laws of Excellent Speech"* found in chapter 13 of this booklet. Take them to heart, because I can assure you, you are being measured by your words.

Adults respect mature behavior. "Conversation" in I Timothy 4:12 speaks of your conduct. Men watch how you behave, how you carry yourself, and how you treat others. They gauge your appropriateness, your manners, and your sincerity. The fastest way to

71

lose the respect of real men is by immature behavior.

Adults respect selfless love. Immaturity is expressed by self love. Maturity is expressed by selfless love. The first great commandment is to wholeheartedly love God, and the second great commandment is to love our neighbor as ourselves. A selfish, self-centered young man is contemptible in the eyes of an adult. However, genuine concern and love for family, for friends, and for the lost will always gain you respect.

Adults respect a good attitude. A good attitude is admired and appreciated by everyone. No one long has patience with a whiner and a complainer! Anyone can see the negative! But a young man who sees the potential positives in every situation will be appreciated.

Adults respect sincere faith. One man said, "Even hypocrites despise hypocrisy!" Yep. If you claim to be a Christian, men will watch to see if you are just talk, or the real deal. No one is perfect, but you can be consistent. The world needs to see authentic Christianity! Anything less, and you will soon be labeled a hypocrite.

Adults respect wholesome purity. How you conduct yourself around ladies will tell other men much about you. Your reputation is and always will be tied to your purity. Never be loose or undisciplined in your behavior towards ladies. Treat all ladies with purity and respect. Look them in the eye or not at all! Be an example of the believer in purity.

If you hope to gain the respect of real men, then learn to be an example of the believer in excellent speech, mature behavior, selfless love, proper attitude, sincere faith, and wholesome purity.

TENET 21

Young men should absorb the wisdom found in the book of Proverbs.

*Proverbs 1:1-4 The proverbs of Solomon the son of David, king of Israel; To know wisdom and instruction; to perceive the words of understanding; To receive the instruction of wisdom, justice, and judgment, and equity; To give subtlety to the simple, to **the young man** knowledge and discretion.*

The opening verses of Proverbs state for us the purpose of its writing. The stated, targeted audience for this collection of wisdom is "the young man". All of us can benefit from its reading, but God is clearly encouraging young men to saturate their souls with its content.

How convenient that the book of Proverbs has been divided into thirty-one chapters! It can easily be read every month by reading just one chapter per day, and an occasional extra chapter on the last day of the month.

Saturate your soul with the Proverbs! Meditate on the wisdom it contains. Ask God to develop your understanding as you seek its depths. From the pages of the Proverbs will come subtlety, strength, discretion, and discernment.

*Proverbs 7:6-8 For at the window of my house I looked through my casement, And beheld among the simple ones, I discerned among the youths, **a young man** void of understanding, Passing through the street near her corner; and he went the way to her house...*

Failing to read the book of Proverbs dooms you to the pitfalls of the "simple ones". Ignorance is deadly! The vast majority of young men are being reared outside of the influence of the Word of

God. Because of this, they are void of understanding, thus easy prey for Satan, as he walks about, "seeking whom he may devour."

Yes, to fail to read the book of Proverbs dooms you to simplicity, but the reading of the book of Proverbs does not guarantee you will become wise! Exposure to wisdom gives you a choice. The fool hears, but despises what he hears. The wise grabs hold of wisdom, internalizes it, and applies it to everyday life.

Proverbs 1:5 A wise man will hear, and will increase learning; and a man of understanding shall attain unto wise counsels:

Proverbs 9:9 Give instruction to a wise man, and he will be yet wiser: teach a just man, and he will increase in learning.

Proverbs 1:7 The fear of the LORD is the beginning of knowledge: but fools despise wisdom and instruction.

My prayer for you is that you will learn to cherish the wisdom that is provided for you in the book of Proverbs. As a young man, it will either protect you against evil, or stand one day as a witness against your simplicity and foolishness.

CONCLUSION

*Ezekiel 22:30 And I sought for a man among them,
that should make up the hedge, and stand in the gap
before me for the land, that I should not destroy it:
but I found none.*

Biblical Masculinity is achieved by adhering to a code of honor. This code is derived from Bible principles, not from the world's perverse definition of manhood.

To a real man, this code is sacred. To break this code is to forsake your honor and disgrace your God. A real man would rather die than do either. Read carefully the code of honor below. It flows from the twenty-one tenets contained in this booklet, and provides for every man a template of Biblical masculinity.

For my God, and upon my honor...

...I will develop an enthusiastic work ethic, and embrace opportunities to use my youthful strength in the performance of physical labor.

...I will master a marketable, wage-earning skill by seeking apprenticeship under skilled men so that I can be a contributor to society, and not a burden.

...I will live courageously by conquering my fears, trusting in God, and performing my duty.

...I will never abuse an assigned position of authority by using it for selfish gain or self-gratification. Instead, I will see every leadership assignment as an opportunity to bring glory to God and to provide service to others.

...I will develop proper communication skills so that I can be trusted to convey a message with accuracy, courtesy, and respect.

...I will not hesitate to draw my sword against evil, and will stand with Godly authority and against those who despise it.

...I will treasure the counsel of older men, and refuse the counsel of those who are immature and foolish.

...I will unashamedly lift up my voice in praise to my God.

...I will wait upon the Lord, seeking His supernatural strength and divine wisdom so that I might better accomplish my duties.

...I will remember my Creator in the days of my youth, and embrace the blessedness of that relationship.

...I will seek my Spirit vision by seeking the fullness of God's Spirit and by listening to His divine leading in my daily life.

...I will be open and accepting to the chance that God might call me into the Gospel ministry. If so, I will embrace it, and if not, I will join myself to a ministry led by a man who is called of God.

...I will seek to master the four disciplines of Christian maturity — disciplined thinking, reputable living, pure convictions, and excellent speech.

...I will seek to master the three vital masculine skills — overcoming Satanic attacks, developing spiritual strength, and internalizing Scriptural truth.

...I will face and defeat my giants, with God's help.

...I will abstain from all forms of fornication, uncleanness, inordinate affection, evil concupiscence, and covetousness.

...I will master the art of chivalry, living always with honor towards women, the aged, children, the weak, and those in need.

...I will wait for God's perfect will in a mate, and will discover all the pleasures of women through one woman, the wife of my youth.

...I will gladly bear the yoke in my youth, and refuse any unequal yoke that would bind me to worldly or devilish influence.

...I will gain the respect of older men by exhibiting stellar character through excellent speech, mature behavior, selfless love, a good attitude, sincere faith, and wholesome purity.

...I will spend much time reading and studying the Bible, especially the book of Proverbs.

If you choose to enter into this sacred covenant with God, then the line provided above is for your signature. This should be done privately, after much consideration. This choice should be a quiet, resolute decision of your mind, your heart and your will.

As you have learned, the transition from boyhood to manhood is not an easy one. Real men do not seek the easy way. God's standard is high, yet we are mortal men. At times you will fail, but you must never, never quit. At times you will fall, but you must get back up. Men — *real men* — learn to overcome failures and setbacks.

Four decades ago, my father started a rural church in a borrowed living room. Within a few years the church had multiplied, prospered and continues to this day to be a strong, stable, soul-winning church. When asked the secret of this success, he spent much time crediting God and giving Him the glory. He then added this piece of advice: "To build anything that will stand the test of time, you must reach *men* for Christ. I appreciate our ladies, love the children, and am glad for our teenagers — but if a ministry is to succeed and prosper, you must reach and disciple *men*."

I pray you will rise to the challenge. Your church, your family, your community and your nation needs you. So, for God's glory and for your own good, be a man!

About the Author

With the writing of this book, Pastor Jerry Ross celebrates thirty-two years of working with young people. He is the senior pastor of the Blessed Hope Baptist Church, in Jasonville, Indiana, an author, and Bible conference speaker.

Other Titles by the Author
www.stayinthecastle.com

The Teenage Years of Jesus Christ
Stay in the Castle
The Seven Royal Laws of Courtship
Is Your Youth Group Dead or Alive?
Grace Will Lead Me Home
The 21 Tenets of Biblical Masculinity
Developing a Teen Soul Winning Program
Parent Appreciation Night

Soon to be released by the author:

The Childhood Years of Jesus Christ
104 Teen Training Hour Lessons — Vol. 1
104 MORE Teen Training Hour Lessons — Vol. 2
The 21 Tenets of Biblical Femininity (by Jerry & Sheryl Ross)

Ultimate Goal Publications
Jasonville, Indiana

www.stayinthecastle.com

(812) 665-4375